OUR WORLD IN COLOUR

GARHWAL AND KUMAON

GARHWAL AND KUMAON

Photography by Ashok Dilwali
Text by Sanjeev Saith

The Guidebook Company Limited

Text and captions by Sanjeev Saith
All photographs by Ashok Dilwali except Sanjeev Saith 8-9, 10-11, 14 (top), 24, 26, 27, 34 (bottom left), 36 (bottom two), 46 (top), 47 (bottom three), 48 (both), 49 (top), 51 (both), 58 (top), 59 (bottom), 60 (all three), 61 (both), 62 (bottom), 67 (top and left), 70 (both), 74 (both) and Toby Sinclair 12.

Editor: David Clive Price
Series Editor: Caroline Robertson
Designed by TC Design
Created by Gulmohur Press, New Delhi

Production House: Twin Age Ltd, Hong Kong

Printed in China

ISBN 962-217-229-6

(title spread)
Trishul peak, 7120 metres (23,3(feet), as seen from Gwaldam. Trishul, first climbed in 1907, is one of the southern ring of peaks that bar access to the inner sanctuary of Nanda Devi.

(right)
A Bhotia lady, in the Pithoragarh district of Kumaon, bordering Tibet, wearing the traditional ceremonial dress on the festival o, Maha-Shivratri at Dharchula. In winter the Bhotias migrate to homes at lower altitudes thus escaping the harsh winters. In summer they take their flocks to higher pastures. Before the 1962 Indo-Chinese border conflict they used to trade across the border with Tibet. A limited amount of trade was restarted with the opening of a new border post in 1992.

(page 6-7)
The Bhairav devta, a form of Shiva, is the guardian deity at Kedarnath. Kedarnath, in the Garhwal Himalayas is one of the many abodes of Shiva and one of the least often visited. Located slightly above the temple, the Bhairav deity has a commanding view of the valley and the Mandakani river that flows from the glacier. Also near the temple i Shankaracharya's samadhi (memorial).

(pages 8-9)
The rich and fertile valley of the Kosi river enroute to Kausani in Kumaon.

(pages 10-11)
The daily arti, offerings to the Ganga at Har-ki-pauri (at the fee of the Lord) at Hardwar. Held every morning and evening with much reverence to the sacred rive which enters the plains here.

(page 12 below)
Although Nainital has expanded considerably since this late nineteenth century map was draw the lake, or tal, remains the focus of the town. Surrounded by hills, the town is today a popular hill resort and centre for numerous public schools.

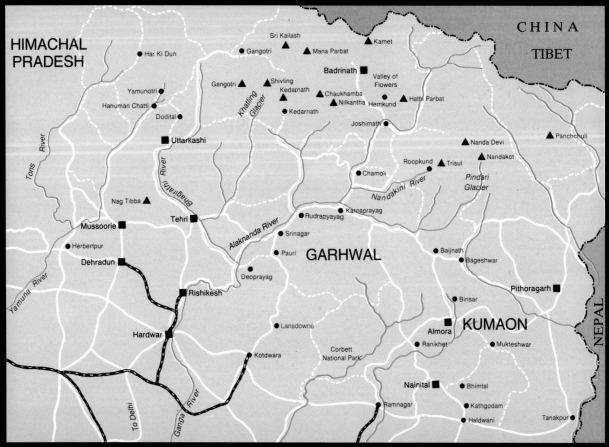

NAINI TAL
AND ENVIRONS

FOR AN INDIAN, A VENTURE INTO THE HIMALAYAS is more than a mere journey; it is a *yatra*—a pious resolve, a celebration of faith or a participation in tradition. For thousands of years, mortal feet have etched out the route of the pilgrim to make the symbolic crossing of Bhavsagar—the Sea of Suffering—through terrain that almost seems to defy man. Nowhere does such a pilgrimage hold more significance than in Garhwal and Kumaon, once known as Uttarakhand, the 'northern territories' of the pre-Vedic era. This is the domain of the ascetic Lord Shiva, the destroyer and re-creator; it is a land charged with shakti, the power and energy of the goddess Parvati, consort of Shiva and daughter of Himavat, Lord of the Mountains. Here, every feature is symbolic of the games that the gods played to create the world. For those who believe, its mountains are the manifestations of the all-powerful Shivling, its streams the flowing form of benevolent goddesses. For others, it is simply a place of rare beauty: reservoir of snows, birthplace of rivers, cradle of peace.

Garhwal and Kumaon together form a substantial wedge in the Central Himalayas, linking Himachal Pradesh in the west to Nepal in the east. Garhwal stretches north from the edge of the Indo-Gangetic plain to the high-altitude cold desert of Tibet, taking in its stride the swell of the Great Himalayan range, which soars here to over 25,000 feet. Perennial rivers, as old as the mountains, rush and foam in the deep gorges that they have carved through these crests over millions of years. It is not surprising that centuries ago, these narrow defiles and remote, elevated valleys became the refuge of the ascetic saints, those who searched for a clear, pure note in the silence. In this complex mosaic of ridgeline and waterway were born cults of mystic Hinduism, the repositiories of which are the isolated mountain shrines scattered along the lesser Himalayas. The classic Hindu scriptures, the Vedas and Shastras, as well as the great epic of the *Mahabarata*, were all conceived in these retreats by ancient religious scholars. Here, if anywhere, could their meditations pass undisturbed. Garhwal today remains a treasure-chest of myth and legend, where every stone tells a story.

Kumaon, lying mostly south of the Great Himalayan range, is more gentle in character. The lie of its land is softer in its undulations, its lore more lyrical. What pervades the open valleys is a simpler, singular faith in the presiding deity of Kumaon—Nanda Devi, the Goddess of Bliss. An incarnation of Parvati, she is manifest in the towering summit of the bewitchingly beautiful mountain named after her. Visible from almost everywhere in Kumaon, the graceful peak of Nanda Devi is said to represent the icy, unmoving form of Parvati in endless expectation of her desired consort, Lord Shiva.

The earliest historical references to the region are found in the Vedas, paeans to the purity of the Himalayas. Specific mention of the mountains exists in the *Mahabarata*, dated to about 1000 BC, when the protagonists of the epic, the Pandavas, are said to have ended their life on earth by ascending the slopes of a peak in western Garhwal called Swargarohini—literally, the 'Ascent to Heaven'. The epic also refers to this region as the home of the Kirata, Pulinda and Tangara tribes. These were probably tribal republics—*janapads*—similar to those that existed in other parts of the western Himalayas. Developed from early settlements of Kol migrants, who were pushed into the hills by the growing Indus Valley Civilisation between 3000 and 1750 BC, and the Khasas—of Aryan origin, who penetrated the Himalayas from the northwest around 2000 BC—these republics are believed to have flourished with distinct cultural identities under

13

(above)*Temple flags rise above a small shrine beside the track between Gangotri and Gaumukh, in Garhwal.*

(below)*Nanda Kot in Kumaon catches the first rays of the morning sun.*

elected or hereditary chiefs. Following the Macedonian march across the Himalayan foothills, an imperialist tradition was established by the Guptas around 330 AD, succeeded by that of the Vardhanas in the fifth century AD. The eventual collapse of the Vardhana empire saw the emergence of a number of small principalities controlled by petty chiefs. These were subject to change in size and power as further waves of migration took place during the time of the Turkish onslaught on the plains. The rigours of the terrain, however, prevented any one ruler from gaining complete control over the whole region. Around the 13th and 14th centuries, a number of forts dotted the hillsides. To the west the Panwars ruled; to the east, the Katyuris and the Chands. King Ajai Pal consolidated 52 of the western fortresses (*garhs*) in the 15th century. A name was given to this unification of *garhs*—Garhwal. Ajai Pal originally based his capital at Joshimath, then Dewalgarh and finally, after stabilising his power, at Srinagar. The land to the east retained its separate identity and came to be known as Kumaon, perhaps a derivation of 'Kumuh', the ancient name that the Khasas gave to their land.

At the end of the 18th century, both Kumaon and Garhwal were overrun by Amar Singh Thapa, the commander of the Gurkha army, in an endeavour to expand the limits of Nepalese territory. The British, who by then had gained supremacy over the plains of northern India, were not amused by this intrusion. Predictably, the Anglo-Gurkha War was fought and by 1815 the Gurkhas were conclusively pushed back into Nepal, while the British annexed most of Garhwal and Kumaon. What followed was equally predictable—a century of exploration of the fascinating Kumaon and Garhwal Himalayas by intrepid British adventurers; the entire region was surveyed, mapped and brought under the central administration. In 1947, India gained independence, and soon both Garhwal and Kumaon were integrated into the northern state of Uttar Pradesh.

Throughout these centuries of political and cultural change what has endured is the undiluted awe that the inhabitants have felt for the Himalayas. Whoever was in power added to the tradition of meditation and worship in these unspoilt mountain enclaves. Today, if a resident is queried about the history of the region, the answer is more likely to be influenced by myth than by chronicle. Even now, the local villages associate various towns and habitations with sacred legend rather than with affairs of state and politics. This is largely due to the efforts of the saint, Adi Shankaracharya, a Namboodri brahmin from Malabar in South India. He was almost single-handedly responsible for the revivalist movement of Hinduism in the early ninth century. At the time that he embarked on his reformist mission, Uttarakhand was a religious patchwork of mystic cults, *naga* worship, tantric rites and animistic faiths. His arduous quest to revitalise the region took him on a pilgrimage to the sources of the sacred rivers of North India. By virtue of his remarkable organisational energy, he succeeded in establishing a series of *dhams* and *maths*—seats of Hindu religion—at elevated sites in the lap of the Himalayas, surrounded by shining summits believed to be the abode of the gods. At Jyotirmath, now Joshimath, he founded an institution of Hindu learning and instruction, a tradition that continues till this day. At Badrinath, he installed the image of Lord Vishnu near the source of the Alaknanda River, and at Kedarnath he chose to enshrine Lord Shiva himself. He died at Kedarnath in AD 820, and his *samadhi* (memorial) draws thousands of pilgrims to this day.

The guru's efforts were rewarded by a following that has continued to grow over the centuries. Subsequent rulers and devotees have added to the

hams and temples, and today there are several pilgrimage routes linking the sacred mountain shrines. Trod by millions of feet over the centuries, these pathways have an unique aura and resonance. Indeed, a devout Hindu will not consider his mortal journey fulfilled until his eyes have witnessed the mountain light on the *dhams* of Uttarakhand.

The pilgrim's progress to the four most sacred *dhams* of Uttarakhand is made along rivers that have shaped the lives of countless millions of North Indians over the centuries: the temple of Yamunotri lies at the head of the River Yamuna; the Ganga is worshipped at Gangotri, where Ganga is said to have descended in a torrent from the heavens; Lord Shiva's shrine at Kedarnath is near the source of the Mandakini River; Badrinath is situated below the massif where the Alaknanda gathers its headwaters. Tradition dictates that a pilgrim should visit these *dhams* from left to right—geographically, from west to east—touching Yamunotri, Gangotri, Kedarnath and Badrinath in that order.

The temple of Yamunotri is situated at 3,185 metres, below Kalinda Parvat, on the left bank of the Yamuna. This slender stream, crystal-clear in its infancy, has travelled a couple of kilometres from its birthplace in the frozen lake of Saptarishi Kund. The daughter of Surya (the sun) and Sangya (consciousness), Yamuna is accepted as being fickle-minded, a trait born of the fact that Sangya was never able to look directly into the dazzling eyes of her husband. Perhaps this is why this temple, too, falls into disrepair every few years and needs to be coaxed back into shape. The idol of Yamuna inside is of black marble, and she is worshipped as the twin sister of Yama, God of Death. Anyone who has bathed in her waters at Yamunotri is spared a tortuous end. The Yamuna still retains a distinct identity in Uttarakand, merging with the Ganga much lower in the plains, at Allahabad.

Ganga, the most sacred of all rivers, is central to the Hindu order of life. Her source is known as Gomukh—the Mouth of the World—visible in our era as the snout of the Gangotri glacier (4,255 metres, or 13,914 feet). This source has since retreated by over 18 kilometres (11 miles) from Gangotri, the ancient site where the Ganga descended from heaven in response to the forceful appeal of King Bhagirath—his ancestors had been reduced to ashes by the wrath of the sage Kapila, whose meditations they had rudely interrupted. Only the goddess Ganga could ensure the salvation of their souls by cleansing their ashes with her pure waters. Bhagirath's intense and determined austerities forced Ganga to descend from heaven in the form of a raging torrent. The force of her cascading waters would have crushed the earth but for the timely intervention of Lord Shiva himself, who absorbed the power of the falling waters with his head, gathered them in his long matted locks, and then released them as gentle streams across Uttarakand. All the rivers and streams of the region are thus considered as forms of the holy Ganga herself, and in fact they unite again through a series of confluences—the *prayags*. Aptly, the Hindu lexicon expresses its gratitude to King Bhagirath by giving a local name to the Ganga in the vicinity of Gangotri. Until she is met by the Alaknanda at Deoprayag, she is known as the Bhagirathi.

Gangotri—Ganga-uttri ('Ganga descended')—has a silver image of the goddess enshrined in a stone temple (3,046 metres, or 9,960 feet) that was constructed by Amar Singh Thapa, the Gurkha commander. The Hindu faith in Garhwal was fortunate to be enhanced even by invaders. A cascade of 30 metres over rocks sculpted by the water serves as a memory of the celestial fall. A small settlement of cottages nearby is a seasonal refuge for monks and pilgrims. Many continue on to the present site of Gomukh, a gentle walk in two stages through

Shivling peak at 6543 metres (21,466 feet), one of the most impressive peaks in the Garhwal Himalaya, rises above the Gangotri glacier.

(above)*A Kumaoni villager spins wool from his sheep in Jatoli enroute to the Sundardhunga glacier.*

(below)*A Garhwali woman near Yamunotri.*

some amazing terrain. From the source emerges the Bhagirathi, not as a trick but already as a river. Above the mammoth glacier towers the phallic massif of Mt Shivling (6,543 metres, or 21,395 feet).

The temple at Kedarnath (3,584 metres, or 11,720 feet) is believed to be over 1,000 years old. That it has retained its austere beauty over so many Himalayan winters is a tribute to its architects. The greystone structure rests on a rectangular base, and is indeed magnificent in its setting. Occupying an airy space in the expansive valley of the upper Mandakini, it has as its backdrop the spectacular mountain summits of Kedarnath (6,940 metres, or 22,694 feet) and its satellite peaks. Inside the temple is the sanctum of Lord Shiva, worshipped here in the form of a curiously shaped rock. Legend has it that the Pandavas (victors of the battle of the *Mahabarata*), having killed kith and kin in the strife, sought redemption from Lord Shiva for their sin of fratricide. Shiva had no desire to grant them absolution and led them on a long chase through the Himalayas, eventually assuming the form of a buffalo to escape from their persistence. Bhim, however, succeeded in identifying the lord amidst a herd. Shiva sank into the ground but Bhim, being of legendary strength, managed to hold on to the hindquarters of the disappearing buffalo. The animal form was torn apart, and only the rump remained with Bhim. Lord Shiva was pleased by this dogged, if audacious devotion. He relented, granting the brothers his blessings. The site of his benediction is Kedarnath, the holiest of Shiva's shrines in the Himlayas, with its petrified rocky form of a buffalo rump. However, there are four other places in Garhwal where parts of the fragmenting buffalo surfaced: the belly at Madmaheshwar, the arms at Tungnath, the face at Rudranath, and the matted locks at Kalpeshwar. Together, these five temple sites constitute the Panch Kedar, the intensive high-altitude mountain pilgrimage for devout Shaivites.

The Vaishnavite, or the worshipper of Lord Vishnu (a known appellation of Badri), embarks on a different circuit—the Panch Badri—of which Badrinath is the premier location. Badrinath (3,096 metres, or 10,124 feet) is the Himalayan seat of Vishnu, reputedly established by Adi Shankaracharya after he learnt through a divine visitation that an idol of the lord was lying submerged in the nearby lake of Narad Kund. He retrieved the black stone idol and enshrined it at the temple of Badrinath. The features of the image have been eroded by prolonged submersion; Vishnu is shown seated in a *padmasana* or lotus posture, a form of iconography not common to Vishnu but to Lord Buddha, his ninth incarnation (Budhhist influence pervaded this region when trade flourished on the Himalayan passes leading to Tibet). The temple, now heavily restored, overlooks the River Alaknanda—known here as the Vishnu Ganga—as it flows south in its valley between the twin peaks of Nar and Narayan to the east and west. High above, beyond Narayan Parbat, rises Nilkantha (6,596 metres, or 21,569 feet), a summit more than 3,000 metres (9,810 feet) above the shrine, though only eight kilometres (five miles) away. Sunrise here is an ethereal spectacle, with the peak above glowing red in the first rays of the sun as if lit by an inner flame, while the valley below is still sunk in shadow. Unlike the Panch Kedar, the Panch Badri are all situated in deep valleys. Yogdhyan Badri, Bhavishya Badri, Vriddha Badri and Adi Badri are all located in the vicinity of Joshimath, which itself houses the Narasingh Badri, the winter abode of Lord Badrinath. The arm of the idol at Narasingh Badri is withering away, growing thinner by the year. It is believed that when the arm actually falls off, the mountains guarding the approach to Badrinath will follow suit. The valley of the main shrine will no longer be accessible, and Lord Vishnu will thereafter be worshipped at Bhavishya Badri—the 'Badrinath of the Future'. Curiously, a spring near Bhavishya Badri is said to be increasing its flow as the arm of Narasingh at Joshimath continues to atrophy.

Each stage in the journey to these *dhams* has its own special history, and local priests willingly recount the legends associated with the various places. Most hallowed along the route are the five *prayags*, the confluences of the holy rivers. At each juncture, the flowing forms of the goddesses unite, eventually giving birth to an even greater energy—the River Ganga. The highest of the confluences is at Vishnuprayag, where the Vishnu Ganga meets the Dhauli Ganga below Joshimath. The only dwelling here is the temple itself, since the steep walls of the canyon deny greater foothold to man. Further downstream, the Alaknanda is met by the Nandakini, which gathers its headwaters from the snows of the sentinel peaks around Nanda Devi.

Nandprayag, where the waters mingle, is named after Nand, Lord Krishna's foster father, who was granted his desire to beget a son like Vishnu. Karnaprayag, marking the union of the Alaknanda with the Pindar, is where Karna, the tragic hero of the *Mahabarata*, acquired his impregnable armour from the sun-god; the Pindar Valley offers passage to Kumaon. The Mandakini, flowing down from Kedarnath, is the first major river to meet the Alaknanda from the west. The confluence is named Rudraprayag, after the eternal ascetic Shiva (known in his enraged aspect as Rudra). A long flight of steps leads to the vantage point from where one can get an ideal view of the junction of the rivers. Deoprayag, the biggest of the five major confluences, is also considered the holiest. Here the Bhagirathi and the Alaknanda, carrying the waters once dispersed by the locks of Shiva, reunite to form the Ganga. Although the Alaknanda carries more volume, its jade-green waters change course dramatically as they meet those born of Gomukh; an assertion, perhaps, of the turbulent Bhagirathi's mission— carrying the mythical ashes of the sage Bhagirath's ancestors to the sea. Deoprayag offers not merely an evocative view, but an opportunity to participate in the divine creation: a natural tongue of rock protrudes from the canyon wall at the point of confluence; steps, carved by man and sculpted by water, lead into the swirl where pilgrims hang on to chains as they immerse themselves in the rushing Ganga, now twice born.

The Ganga, in full flow, hurries through the last lap of its mountainous course before it enters the plains at Hardwar. The name of this sacred city means the 'Gates of Heaven', for it is here that all pilgrimages to the mountain shrines traditionally begin. Each day, thousands of devotees pass through its portals, stopping to bathe at Har-ki-pauri, the holy *ghats* that bear the footprint of Shiva. And having washed, they find a quiet spot on the steps to wait for the gathering dark, when they will ritually float flowers and lighted earthen lamps down the water. This is the hour of the *aarti*, the fire worship of the Ganga, for which Har-ki-pauri is renowned. Every 12 years, Hardwar hosts the Kumbh *mela* or fair, when millions of Indians converge on these banks for a dip on the auspicious day. Understandably, the town is really a collection of pilgrim houses—*dharamshalas*—each catering to pilgrims of a particular ethnic group. Conforming to the architecture and ambience of a specific region of India, each pilgrim house offers the comforting familiarity of food and language, as well as the accustomed mode of worship. Scores of assorted temples are littered across the town, which resounds each day to a common prayer uttered in a hundred different dialects.

Perhaps the only place of pilgrimage along the Ganga that derives its character more from the holiness of its living inhabitants than from its

Musicians accompany their local deity to a neighbouring village.

Most of the bigger rivers have their true source in the glaciers of the higher reaches but are joined by small streams that gush and flow into them.

mythical deities is Rishikesh. *Sadhus, swamis* and *rishis*—ascetics in search spiritual excellence—reside along the banks in this city of seminaries upstrea of Hardwar. It is an accepted custom in India for a troubled mind to come Rishikesh in quest of peace. Most of the *ashrams* are institutions that concentra on the teaching of a rigorous spiritual discipline, and have a following th reaches across the barriers of politics and religion. The Kailash Ashran the Divine Life Society, the *ashram* of Maharishi Mahesh Yogi, these a among those that provide refuge to a disturbed soul.

Although it would appear that the *raison d'être* of Uttarakhan is, quite simply, the pilgrimage, the attractions of the land are n diminished in any way once it is stripped of religious associations. The ve qualities that drew gods, sages and scholars to these Himalayan retrea continue to attract others, perhaps in even greater measure, because the natural endowments have been enhanced over the centuries by the growin charm of the local culture. For the contemporary tourist, distanced from th religious circuit, a holiday in these northern territories is a far cry from th sea of sufferings that they represented for the original pilgrim. Today, th 'soft option' is available, with roads leading to most destinations. Kumaon, fact, scores over Garhwal in this respect, with its lower, more stable hillsid offering better travel facilities and some superbly sited towns that a extremely popular for their vistas of the Garhwal Himalaya. Something what the committed pilgrim strives to reach is visible in a 120° panoram from these comfortable viewpoints. Pride of place must go to Binsar (2,41 metres, or 7,887 feet), the hilltop perch with the most stunning view of th Great Himalayan range: from here, the sun can be seen rising over the peak in Nepal and setting over the far end of an uncluttered panorama.

Chosen as the summer retreat of the Chand rulers, Binsar derives i name from the temple of Bineshwar (an aspect of Shiva), built by Raja Kalya Chand. Other towns that provide similar experiences at dawn and dusk a Kausani, Ranikhet, Chaukori, Mukteshwar and Pithoragarh. Ranikhet, a charm ing cantonment, also has a nine-hole golf course on a rolling plateau at 1,80 metres (5,886 feet). Chaukori is the closest to the peaks, the summits seemingl within an arm's reach in the clear light of dawn; tea gardens carpet the slopes Chaukori and its neighbouring village, Berinag.

The circuit of hill roads linking these viewpoints dips into pictur esque valleys with some ancient sites of architectural and historical interes Jageshwar is a temple complex dating back to the eighth and ninth centuries A comprising over 150 shrines in the *shikhara* style, and set in a narrow riverin valley enveloped by tall deodars. Baijnath, in the idyllic Garur Valley, has ancien temples dedicated not only to Shiva and Parvati, but also to Ganesh, Kuber, Sury and Brahma. The oldest shrine in this complex was built in the 12th century Priceless stone carvings can be seen in the Baijnath Museum next to the temple besides which the green waters of the Gomti flow. Patal Bhuvaneshwar offers surreal experience—a complex maze of underground caves serrated with fang like stalactites and stalagmites. Some chambers are large enough to host a orchestral performance. Another site that fires the imagination is Lakhu-Udya the 'red cave'. This hood-like rocky shelter has prehistoric blood-coloure frescoes that portray the early inhabitants of Kumaon as hunters with bows an arrows, living amidst pines. In one depiction, a human figure, sword in hand, about to sacrifice another.

Of course, some places attract visitors purely by virtue of thei climatic charms and ambience. Referred to simply as 'hill stations'

Mussoorie and Nainital are two such cities, catering in prime time to a floating population that outstrips the residents, but maintaining a certain popularity throughout the year. Alpine cottages, shopping promenades, recreational centres, restaurants and hotels cling to the Himalayan spurs, enveloped by dense woods of oak, pine, fir and rhododendron. The prime attraction of Nainital is the lake that gives the town its name and character; fringed with graceful weeping willows, the emerald waters have quiet walks along their four-kilometre circumference, while a boat club adds to the natural pleasures of the lake, which is named after the eyes (*nain*) of Parvati.

Nainital actually forms the core of what is known as the 'Lake District of Kumaon'. Others in the vicinity are the larger Bhimtal, the complex of Sat-tal (the Seven Lakes) and the nine-cornered Naukuchiya Tal. Each is an idyllic resort with wooded walks along its banks and with yachts and paddleboats to cross the placid waters. These lakes of Kumaon are easy to access, but a visitor has to toil before he can reach the bank of Garhwal's high-altitude pools. Dodital (3,024 metres or 9,888 feet), two days' walk away from the road, is an angler's paradise. This lovely lake, one of the highest places in the world where trout can be found, is surrounded by dense woods and a profusion of flowers in summer. A variety of wild life can be spotted in the late evenings as it descends from the higher reaches to this beautiful waterpoint. Other lakes are even higher. Hemkund (4,150 metres, or 13,570 feet), the 'Lake of Ice', is sacred to the Sikhs; it is believed to be the location where Guru Gobind Singh (the Tenth Guru) meditated before he raised an army to fight the Mughals on the plains, but the superb environs are reason enough to make the pilgrimage. Just off the trek to the famed Valley of Flowers, Hemkund receives a steady stream of visitors, both pilgrims and naturalists. Less frequented is the cluster of seven lakes known as Sahastratal, near the Khatling glacier. As high as 4,572 metres (14,950 feet), these isolated water bodies are the focus of an annual pilgrimage for nearby villagers, who take their ritual dip in the freezing waters. The fortunate are rewarded by a sighting of the Brahmakamal—the exotic Himalayan Lotus—by the water's edge. Perhaps the most enigmatic, and least accessible, is Roopkund (4,778 metres, or 15,624 feet). Only about 150 metres in circumference and quite shallow, this glacial pool thaws during the summer for a few weeks. What attracts most people to its high-altitude location is not merely the fascinating trek through the meadows with their excellent views, but the grisly past. Strewn around it, and even visible on some warm days, are the skeletal remains of about a hundred people believed killed by an avalanche some 500 to 600 years ago. Needless to say, the site has fuelled much speculation about the possible identities of these unfortunate travellers. Who were these intrepid folk, trespassing where nature is no longer kind? Perhaps they too belonged to the cult of Nanda Devi and had ventured into this white expanse to propitiate the goddess, 400 years before the age of the ice-axe.

It is not surprising that people from the West, subject to more prosaic promptings, should begin to wander along the slopes of Nanda Devi. The magic of the bewitching mountain has ensured a devotion bordering on the mystical. British district commissioners, surveyors, publishers, doctors, and of course professional mountaineers, have all succumbed to its lure. Mountaineering as a sport began in the Himalayas in the 19th century—as a quest to reach the feet of the goddess. Today, Garhwal and Kumaon are visited by scores of expeditions from all over the world. This complex knot of the Great Himalayan range is studded with summits whose names ring with reverence:

The first trees bloom in March and April annoucing the end of winter. Throughout the summer different species flower and trails through the hills are lined by a variety of shrubs and trees.

Devprayag, at the confluence of the Alaknanda and Bhagirathi rivers.

Nanda Devi, the Goddess of Bliss (7,817 metres, or 25,562 feet); Trishul, th Trident of Shiva (7,120 metres, or 23,282 feet); Nanda Ghunti, the Veil of th Goddess (6,309 metres, or 20,630 feet); Swargarohini, the Ascent to Heave (6,252 metres, or 20,444 feet); Nilkantha, the Blue-throated Shiva (6,59 metres, or 21,569 feet). There are hundreds of peaks above 6,000 metres, mar unnamed and unclimbed, to challenge those keen on ascending summits. Fc others less driven, who perhaps draw pleasure simply from being in unspoi places in the folds of mountains, the fascinating topography of Uttarakhar holds enough surprises to occupy them for many seasons. Chanelled by th crests and troughs, they may wander over the high, icy passes like pilgrin of a different order.

Recently, a new method of adventure travel has come into vogue in thes valleys. River runners raft down the various arms of the Ganga, using nature own thoroughfare to gain a unique perspective of the land. With the rapic now well read and graded, this guided sport is fast gaining popularity. It is als an interesting method by which to observe the amazing flora ar fauna of the region, away from the more permanent mark of man. S unexpected is human activity in some of these river canyons that barking dee have been known to fall off their delicate perches, surprised by the stealth intrusion of man.

Lower Garhwal and Kumaon are richly endowed with wildlife. Th southernmost fold of the hills—the Shivaliks—rises only abou 1,000 metres (3,270 feet) from the Gangetic flats, and often has another broa plain beyond it, as at Dehradun. Blessed with abundant monsoon rains, th slopes of the Shivaliks are densely forested both with tropical species like sa teak and bamboo, and with more arid thorny scrub as one moves higher. This the preserve of a spectrum of wildlife such as the barking deer, tiger, leopar bear, elephant, and a rich array of birds. The Corbett National Park, one of India finest sanctuaries, is situated here on the banks of the Ramganga. A 'tribute' t an enlightened hunter, the park was named after the legendary Jim Corbett– naturalist, writer and photographer, perhaps best known for his feats of trackin and hunting down the dreaded man-eaters of Kumaon and Garhwal. Corbe National Park, a naturalists' delight, has recorded the presence of 50 mammal 500 birds and 25 reptile species. The Lesser Himalayas north of the Shivaliks a carpeted with magnificent conifers—fir pine, cypress, deodar—as well as oal succeeded by rhododendron and birch in the higher reaches. In these fores there are bears, leopards, musk deer, flying squirrels and some very colourfu avifauna. Still higher, above the treeline, are the *bugyals*, idyllic aplin meadows with clumps of juniper and a riot of wildflowers that push the way out of the thawing soil in spring. A prized specimen is th Himalayan blue poppy. Two such meadows are the Valley of the Flowei (3,658 metres, or 11,962 feet) and Har-ki-dun (3,565 metres, or 11,658 feet both popular destinations for trekkers. Only a few species of Himalaya wildlife enjoy the severe conditions of this alpine zone. There are bhara Himalayan tahr, the lynx, and the elusive snow leopard. Higher still, amon the granites, gneisses and snow, even birds and animals are transient visitor The snow leopard may use a high pass to cross from one valley to anothe and choughs and snow pigeons may occasionally be seen gliding in th thermals above.

That nature in such profusion should make living in its shadow matter of survival is one of life's ironies. The hillfolk who dwell in thes high places live simply, and by the season. With economic developmer still a long way off, Garhwal and Kumaon continue to be backward agraria societies, in which the villagers eke out a frugal livelihood from shepherding and from cultivation of terraced fields that hug the contours of the mountainsides. Over the years, the mounting pressure of population has outpaced the meagre yield of subsistence agriculture, and the local population—especially the menfolk—has begun migrating to serve on the plains. For those who choose to stay behind, life continues in awe of the mountain gods, a life pitifully insignificant against the scale of the Himalayan surroundings.

Living as a community has always been a shared tradition, which is also reflected in cultural expression. Celebration is a collective affair; song and dance are usually performed in groups. The themes are predictable: love, lore and nature. The flute and the *hurka* (an hourglass-shaped drum) are the popular instruments. The beat of the *hurka* is commonly heard in the fields during cultivation, marking time for the collective planting. Ballads— usually heroic ones of struggle and triumph—are sung as a diversion from the chore of survival. Evening is the time for the more soulful and lilting songs of love, and of separation. The *chhopati* are love songs sung by groups of men and women in the form of questions and answers. *Khuded* songs depict the suffering of a wife when her husband leaves the village to look for a job. The *chhura*, sung among the shepherds by the old to the young, is valuable advice drawn from experience, especially in the art of rearing livestock. Folk dances, of course, are a physical expression of celebration. The *jhora* is the most popular, performed by men and women linking arms together and forming a circle. Chains of up to 200 participants dip and sway to the beat of the local orchestra. On a particularly riotous night, the *do-manzila jhora* (the double-decker *jhora*) may be performed, with partners perched on the dancers' shoulders. Although the villagers break into step at the slightest opportunity, the festive occasions for such rejoicing are *Hariyala* (the harvest festival), *Uttaraini* (the winter festival devoted to Lord Shiva) and *Nandashtami* (the most colourful of fairs, held in honour of Nanda Devi). The *chhapeli* is a dance of courtship, while the *chholiya* is a historical wedding dance performed by pairs of men in flowing robes, wielding swords and shields—a relic of the age when marriages were made at the point of a sword. Some dances find their roots in the ancient rituals of spirit worship. The *jagar*, performed at night around a fire, invokes the spirit of the local deity. Accompanied by the mounting frenzy of drums and singing, the ones who serve as the medium become entranced, shivering, shouting and leaping in the ecstasy of possession. Problems that beset the villages are then presented before them, to which they provide solutions. Those entranced are known to perform astonishing feats like eating live coals, licking red-hot pokers, or entering a fire without being harmed. The 22-day-long Byasi dance is believed to have the power to rid the community of epidemics and other natural calamities.

To a visitor it would seem that all these cultural impressions are symbolic of an existence that is sometimes stable, sometimes nomadic, always unpredictable. For those who live in such high places, however, life is a blessing granted to them by the mountain gods and sustained by the vital waters of the Ganga. Serenity comes naturally to these hillfolk, wrapped in the quiet peace of their intimate retreats.

Once on a celestial day in heaven, Lord Shiva raised his voice in song. Vishnu, who was listening, was so moved by the music that he began to flow like water. Brahma, the Creator, collected the pure liquid and named it the Ganga. Aeons later, the will of a mortal king brought this creation of the holy trinity down to Uttarakhand. Today, those who are willing to listen can still hear in the rush of water a divine melody.

(above)*The Swami Naryan Ashram in Pithoragarh district is a three day walk from Tawaghat.*

(below)*Hutton's Cottage, in Nainital, is one of the many summer homes built by the British in Kumaon. Its magnificent garden is one of the finest in Nainital.*

Bhagirathi peaks seen from the route to Gomukh. The highest peak is Bhagirathi 1. The Gangotri glacier can be seen below the peaks. (From the left, the peaks are Bhagirathi 2, 3 and 1.)

Gaurikund is believed to be the spot where the Ganga descended to earth. Geologists believe that the snout of the Gangotri glacier might once have extended to this point.

(facing page)
Gangotri in late winter. Gangotri has a few hundred monks and staff running ashrams, which provide food and shelter to the pilgrims in summer.

(above)*The temple at Tungnath after a fresh snowfall. Tungnath, a Shiva temple, is the highest temple in the Garhwal and Kumaon region. Tungnath is one of the Panch Kedar.*

(below)*The temple at Gangotri after its recent restoration. Seen across the river are some of the ashram cottages run by religious trusts and swamis.*

(above)*A trickle of melting snow falls through
the cold air near Gomukh; on contact with the
glacial surface it creates a gigantic ice
stalagmite.*

(right)*Shivling peak glows in the first rays of
morning. The east ridge, with its conspicuous
pillar, is etched along the left skyline. This
remarkable route was climbed by a team of four
international climbers in 1981.*

(facing page)
(top) *A mule train on its way to Kedarnath. In spring each year, the Kedarnath shrine opens for pilgrims.*
(below) *The old and infirm use mules, palanquins and porters to reach the shrine.*

The temple courtyard has an image of Nandi, Shiva's vahan or vehicle, opposite the temple entrance. Prayers are offered both at the temple and to the nearby Bhairabnath deity.

(left)*The Gurudwara at Hemkund is the highest and probably the most inaccessible in India. The site marks the place where Guru Gobind Singh is believed to have meditated before returning to the plains in order to raise an army against the Mughals. The lake was 'rediscovered' in 1930 by a Sikh soldier on leave, who followed the guru's textual description.*

Kukbhushandi Tal, at almost 4,876 metres (16,000 feet) in the Garhwal, is reached after a three-day walk from Bhyundar, en route to the Valley of Flowers. According to local legend, the sage Kukbhushandi related the epic Ramayana to Lord Garuda on the banks of this half-mile-long lake.

The Sati Ansuya Temple.

(facing page)
The Badrinath Temple above the Alaknanda River in Garhwal. This shrine to Lord Vishnu is considered one of the holiest in India. Until the recent road was built, it was also the most inaccessible. The hot sulphur springs of Tapt Kund may explain the location of this important temple.

The facade of the Badrinath Temple has been restored many times.

Pilgrims take a ritual bath in the hot sulphur springs of Tapt Kund. Souvenirs of the various deities of Uttarakhand, including the Vishnu image, sell in street stalls outside the main temple. The nearby bazaar was recently damaged by an avalanche and then rebuilt.

The Alaknanda and the Mandakini meet at Rudraprayag, which is one of the five important confluences or pryags on the Alaknanda.

Storms in the Himalaya can build up quickly and alter the landscape in a few hours. The temple at Bhaironghati shows the contrast after an unexpected snowfall. The temple is 10 km short of Gangotri.

The route to Roopkund initially moves up the Pindar Valley and climbs high through thinning vegetation to the Bugyals.

(following pages)
The Mandakini is the principal river of Kedarkhand, the abode of Shiva. Emerging from the glaciers below the majestic Kedarnath peaks, it is joined by minor tributaries that flow down from the other places of pilgrimage dotting this region of the Panch Kedar.

Among all the rivers of Uttarakhand, the Alaknanda carries the most volume—until it meets the Bhagirathi at Deoprayag. The rock-carved steps give access to the confluence, where the waters of the two sacred rivers rush together to form the Ganga.

(facing page)
The Kaliganga is one of the numerous streams that meet to form the lower tributaries of the Ganga.

The remarkable yatras of Nanda Devi
are a ritual dramatisation of the post-
marital journeys of newly married
women from their natal village to those
of their husbands. The image of the
goddess is carried on her palanquin in a
spectacular journey from her temple at
Nauti, over the bugyals, past the
mysterious Roopkund, to the base of the
mountain-curtain that surrounds the
peak of Nanda Devi.

*The Bara-Jat yatra occurs every 12
years, when a four-horned ram is
miraculously born and leads the
procession. Smaller pilgrimages are
an annual event.*

(facing page)
In the middle ranges of the central Himalaya rhododendron trees cover whole hillsides and skirt many villages. The magnificent blooms attract numerous bird species for which the Garhwal and Kumaon Himalaya is famous.

The Dogalbitta resthouse is an old favourite of those who frequent Garhwal. It commands an excellent view of the Kedarnath range. Many villages, too, have resthouses (or even schoolhouses) where trekkers can take shelter for the night. A day spent with the villagers as they work in their terraced fields is rewarding.

(above) Rishikesh is the retreat of rishis and munis, the holy and the wise who live a spartan life along its banks.

(left) A dry river bed in the Doon Valley

(facing page)
(top) Pilgrims at the Khujapuri Temple

(middle and bottom right)The residents of the sacred city of Rishikesh are a mix of those who teach, those who have come to learn through the discipline and teachings of the gurus and ashrams, and those who prefer to follow a solitary, individualistic path to knowledge through experience and penance.

(bottom left) The Ganga emerges from the folds of the mountains at this city of ashrams, which is the first major settlement to spread across both its banks. Residents and visitors cross the river by using the famous Laxman Jhula bridge and the ferries that ply a little downstream.

The ghats at the renowned Har-ki-Pairi are the centrum, as it were, of the holy city of Hardwar. Pilgrims come to Hardwar to bathe in the waters of the Ganga at this sacred site. Although the bathing rituals may be conducted in the morning, all converge at the steps in the magic hour of dusk to witness the aarti to the Ganga. Those who sit on the banks and watch the priests conduct this fire-worship also participate by floating flowers and earthen lamps on the water.

Most of Kumaon's lower valleys
are less rugged than Garhwal.
The terracing of its fields, too, is
less convoluted and precarious in
its perch. Harvests are in
comparision, more rewarding
than those in Garhwal.

he open vistas of Kumaon can
easily reached by road.
ausani is among the most
pular tourist destinations.
riving from one spot to another
ovides ample opportunity to
ast on a view like that of the
nse pines east of Almora or the
osaic of fields in the Valley of
e Kosi.

Towards the north and east, however, the
Kumaon Himalaya has challenging terrain.
A classic trek is that to the base of the peak of
Nanda Devi East, in the Pithoragarh district.
The walk is made in the company of porters and
sheep—local carriers all—and leads the trekker
along a track etched on rock, past the ubiqui-
tous temples and shrines on the wayside
dedicated to the goddess. The varying species of
Himalayan flora and fauna add colour and
further beauty to the area.

Nanda Devi East, the lower summit of the Nanda Devi massif, is linked to the main peak by a long and sharp ridge. The eastern peak is accessible from both inside and outside the 'sanctuary', being part of the protective curtain itself. It was first climbed in 1939 by a Polish team, and then ascended again by a French expedition that attempted to traverse the airy ridge between the two summits. The massif, the tallest in the Garhwal and Kumaon, is visible from most parts of the region and presents the varying facets of its character in many different lights.

The forests of Binsar are protected: they have been demarcated as a sanctuary. A variety of fauna live in the preserve and human dwellings are few; those who do live in the handful of cottages on this hill are fortunate to be blessed with such surroundings.

A view of the Garur Valley from the road leading down from Kausani. The valley is a deep bowl, with the Gomti River flowing through it past Baijnath, the main temple in the region.

(above left) *Just 20 kilometres (12 miles) upstream is another famous temple—that of Bagrath, at Bageshwar. Traditionally attired devotees pour water and milk over the Nandi image of Shiva's vahana.*
(above right) *The iconography of these temples as well as the motifs carved on the walls of the group are of particular interest . The Bagrath Temple at Bageshwar also has some ancient and curious icons in its courtyard, such as this one of Lord Ganesh*

(below right) *The Baleshwar group of temples at Champawat are also considered to be of high architectural merit, especially the Ras Mandap .*

(facing page)
At Baijnath, on the banks of the Gomti River, is the ancient temple complex of Baijnath. Dating back to the 13th century AD, the temples are dedicated to Shiva, Parvati, Ganesh and a number of other deities, some of whose icons are seen in the courtyard and in the small museum. Tablets bear inscriptions in the old Kumaoni script of the Katyuri Dynasty, which was responsible for the temple's foundation.

63

(preceding page)
The names of different shrines signify various aspects of Lord Shiva, who is worshipped with abandon during Maha-Shivratri on the no-moon night of the month of Phalgum (February–March).

The temple complex of Jageshwar has over 150 shrines set amidst towering deodars that are perhaps as old as this ancient Shaivite site. They contain superb examples of Chand architectural styles and the doorways are profusely carved in great detail.

(facing page)
'Dandeshwar' is one of the names of Shiva, to whom this temple, a beautiful example of Chand architecture, is dedicated. It is considered part of the Jageshwar complex, just two kilometres away.

The Bhotias are a tribal community that once carried out trade with Tibet. They reveal their links with the Tibetans through their features as well as their culture. Today, they are largely grouped around Dharchula (below). Since trade came to a halt they have been absorbed into the Kumaoni way of life. Here they are dancing during the Shivratri celebrations.

...arriages are simple, though momentous occasions that bring together ...igion, ritual, commerce, music, dance and a dash of history. The devi or ...vta is invoked to bless the couple, the bride and groom are bedecked with ...erings in keeping with the status of the family, the spartan band leads the ...dding procession, and the dancers enact the Chholiya dance, retelling the ...ce-common custom of winning a bride at the point of a sword.

...ollowing page)
...uring Raksha Bandhan each August, the Devi Dhura festival takes place at ...horagarh in Kumaon. The villages wage a ritual battle, hurling stones at ...ch other and offer the drawn blood to the Devi or goddess.

Women in Garhwal and Kumaon do most of the work that sustains a household: tending the fields, collecting firewood, looking after the children, cooking the meal. Wider access to education through middle-level schools in each village may help to change these conventions and bring working women into the mainstream.

One of the features of houses throughout the Himalaya are the carved wooden doors, door frames and windows. Many, such as these near Almora, are painted.

(facing page)
Despite heavy deforestation and changes in land use along the length of the Himalaya there are still some ares of unspoilt mountain grassland and montane forest.

Bhimtal is the largest lake in the region and is named after Bhim, one of the five Pandava brothers, heroes of the epic Mahabharata.

(above) A temple dedicated to him is situated at the water's edge.
(below) The lake resort has facilities for fishing and boating, along with limited accommodation.

(facing page)
Naukuchiya Tal (above) and Khurpa Tal (below) are the two other lakes that together form Kumaon's 'Lake District'. The nine-cornered Naukuchiya Tal is the smallest and the surrounding woods are famous for their range of bird species. Khurpa Tal is the nearest to Nainital and is a lovely sight when seen from above, surrounded by a patchwork of fields and cottages.

(above)*The first rays of morning light up the water's edge at Nainital. Fringed with trees through which a track circles the lake, the tal is surrounded by seven hilltops offering beautiful views of the Himalaya and the town.*

(below) *view of Nainital from China Peak.*

(facing page)
The Church of St John-in-the-Wilderness is one of the earliest buildings in Nainital and its impressive stained glass make it one of the finest churches in any hill station.

Corbett National Park protects a large area of the Shivalik foothills of the Himalaya and falls in both Kumaon and Garhwal.

(following page)
Pindari Glacier

ALMORA (1,646m) This hill station was founded by Raja Kalyan Chand in 1560 AD; its pictureseque location along the saddle of a ridge has ensured a steady flow of visitors. A kilometre's walk takes one up to the Kasar Devi Temple, which has an excellent view of the Himalayas.

BAGESHWAR (915m) Situated at the confluence of the Gomti and Saryu rivers, this is an ancient pilgrim centre containing the Bagnath Temple dedicated to Shiva. Thousands converge here in January on the occasion of the Uttaraini fair in order to have a dip at the prayag. Bageshwar is also the base for treks to the Pindari, Kafni and Sunderdunga glaciers.

CHAMPAWAT (1,615m) Once the capital of the Chand Dynasty, this quiet town is renowned for the architectural beauty of the Baleshwar temple complex and the Ratneshwar Champawati Durga temples.

CHITAI Eight kilometres away from Almora is the Gaur Bhairav Temple dedicated to Gollu Devta, a local deity much loved by the Kumaonis. Hundreds of bells are strung in chains around the temple—all donations from devotees whose prayers have been fulfilled.

DEHRADUN Situated on a broad plain between the Shivaliks and the lesser Himalayas, this 'halting place in the valley' is a city of schools. In addition to hosting some of the premier private institutions in the country (such as the Doon School and Welham's), the Indian Military Academy is to be found here. The peaceful environs of the valley have also attracted those in search of tranquillity and a temperate climate, with the result that the city now has a large resident population of retired civil servants.

GAUCHER On the map by virtue of its large flats that are used by VIPs for landing their small planes and helicopters, this little town comes to life in the years when it hosts a trade fair. Visitors from all parts of Uttarkashi flock to these grounds for both commerce and merry-making—a tradition that has continued for hundreds of years, ever since the days when the fair was also an exhibition of goods from distant Tibet.

GWALDAM An idyllic town, Gwaldam is set amidst thick pine woods and apple orchards that extend to the adjoining hilltops. Positioned against a backdrop of the Trisul and Nanda Ghunti peaks, it is the starting point for some of the most popular treks in Garhwal.

HOT WATER SPRINGS The presence of therapeutic hot water springs along the pilgrim paths is a blessing to weary travellers. Yamunotri and Badrinath are well frequented spots that have soothing waters in which to bathe. Others are at Gaurikund (en route to Kedarnath) and Gangnani (on the way to Gangotri).

KATARMAL (1,554m) This hill near Almora is renowned for its 800-year-old temple dedicated to the sun. A short walk away are the woods of Bikut, from which the saddle of Almora can be viewed.

LAKHAMANDAL This village derives its name from the legend of Lakhamandir or Lakshagriha — the Shellac Palace. The five Pandava brothers, victors of the epic battle of the Mahabharat, were lured to spend time in this exquisite firetrap. Once inside, the *palace of lac* was set ablaze by their adversaries, the Kauravas. The Pandavas, however, were wise to the plot and escaped through an underground tunnel. The remains of this palace as well as a beautiful 8th century Madhu Mahadev temple draw visitors to the small village — a ropebridge away from Kuan in the Yamuna valley.

MILAM GLACIER 27 kilometres from névé to snout, this is the longest glacier in the Garhwal and Kumaon Himalayas. A 54 kilometre trek over 5 days takes one through some interesting villages to the snout of the glacier, which is the source of the Gori Ganga. Milam village, nearest the glacier, is one of the highest in the range.

MUKTESHWAR This charming town, 59 kilometres from Nainital, is famous for its apples and its view. Sited at 2,286 metres on a junction of the Gagar and Lohukhet ridges, Mukteshwar presents a panoramic view of the Garhwal and Kumaon Himalayas. The Indian Veterinary Research Institute, established in 1898, is located here.

NAG TIBBA Two days of walking takes one up to this hilltop at 3,048 metres. The peak is named after Nag Deota (the snake God), and the local villagers gather here to seek protection for their cattle from the deity. The walk along the ridge has panoramic views of over 200 miles of the Great Himalayan Range.

NARENDRANAGAR The summer capital of Maharaja Narendra Singh of Tehri, this township is centred around his palace and is perched on a ridge at 1,173m. The location, surrounded by forests, provides a beautiful view of the Ganga as it enters the plains near Rishikesh. The palace once housed exquisite miniature paintings.

PINDARI GLACIER The six day 57 kilometre trek to this Himalayan glacier has been one of the most frequented routes in the region. The beautiful walk has five convenient night halts en route, each with a PWD resthouse, a facility that has enhanced its popularity. The glacier is situated below the outer curtain of the Nanda Devi Sanctuary. The snout of the glacier is at a height of 3,656 metres and is best visited in May–June and September–October.

RAWAL The priest at Badrinath is known as the Rawal. Like Adi Guru Sankaracharya, he is a Namboodri Brahman from Kerala. Fluent in Sanskrit, ritual, and the religious scriptures, he is appointed by the Temple Committee and the former Maharaja of Tehri Garhwal. Celibacy is one of the necessary qualifications, and he ceases to be Rawal if he marries.

SRINAGAR Once the ancient capital of Garhwal, and perhaps still its cultural capital, Srinagar lies on the banks of the Alaknanda as it flows through the widest valley in the region. Quite apart from being the home of medieval temples and the Garhwali School of Miniature Painting, Srinagar today also boasts the University of Garhwal.

TEHRI Tehri was built in the early 19th century by Maharaja Sudarshan Shah of Garhwal after the British an nexed his erstwhile capital, Srinagar, as indemnity for the Anglo-Gurkha War. Situated at the confluence of the Bhilangana and the Bhagirathi, the town is frequented largely because it lies at the junction of routes to Uttarkashi, Rishikesh, Deoprayag and Srinagar. Currently its fate is linked to that of the Tehri dam, which will be the largest in Asia when completed. Tehri itself will then become a memory, since it will be submerged by the reservoir.

TRIJUGINARAIN Lying on the ancient bridle path between Gangotri and Kedarnath, this village is considered to be the site of the wedding of Shiva and Parvati. A fire in the front portico of the temple of Vishnu has been burning for hundreds of years, a relic of the sacred ritual.

UTTARKASHI The first town along the course of the Bhagirathi to spread either side of the river, this night-halt en route to Gangotri is the 'Kashi of the North'. Like Varanasi on the plains, it houses the Vishwanath Temple among others. For some seekers, the pilgrimage ends in this town—at the Nehru Institute of Mountaineering, which trains hundreds of young climbers every year.

VASUDHARA FALLS Many pilgrims continue beyond Badrinath to the Vasudhara Falls, 6 kilometres away, where the Vishnu Ganga drops over a 122 metre step. With a captivating backdrop of rock and snow, the waterfall is spectacular. Chaukhamba, Satopanth, and Balakun are among the Himalayan summits that loom over the valley.

About the photographer:
Ashok Dilwali has already published six earlier photographic books on different regions of the Himalaya including a companion volume to this, together with Sanjeev Saith, on Himachal Pradesh. He has held exhibitions of photographs in New Delhi, where between trips to the Himalaya, he manages to run a family owned photographic business. Ashok Dilwali was recently awarded and became an Associate of the Royal Photographic Society of Great Britain, London.

About the author:
Sanjeev Saith has managed to combine a career as a photographer and writer with his passion for the mountains. He has participated in many climbs, rafting expeditions and long treks throughout the Himalaya over the last twenty years. He has had photographic exhibitions in London, New Delhi and Bombay. His film on the India Everest Expedition was judged best documentary at the 1985 National Film Festival. His books include *A Journey Down the Ganga and Our World in Colour Himachal Pradesh*. Sanjeev Saith has a Master's degree in Economics, and lives in New Delhi.